Jo

Thanks for keeping me ~~travelled feet~~ safe, the convos + support

Enjoy, you'll laugh, cry + be inspired

(also makes for ~~a~~ good paper aeroplanes)

**Also in this series of new poetry and fiction from LinguaBooks**

No Means No
The Legend of Sidora
The Taste of Rain
A Parting Shot
Tales from Happy Valley

# Belongings

Poetry from a kaleidoscopic mind

Wayne Martyn

**LinguaBooks**
www.linguabooks.com

All rights reserved. No part of this publication may be reproduced, stored in a retrieval system or transmitted, in any form or by any means, electronic, mechanical, photocopying, recording or otherwise, without the prior permission of the publishers.

Print edition: ISBN 978-1-911369-60-8
eBook edition: ISBN 978-1-911369-61-5

First edition

Editor: Ann Claypole

Copyright © 2024 LinguaBooks

A CIP catalogue record for this book is available from the British Library.

Wayne Martyn has asserted his right under the Copyright, Designs and Patents Act, 1988 to be identified as the author of this work.

This book is sold subject to the condition that it shall not, by way of trade or otherwise, be lent, resold, hired out or otherwise circulated without the publisher's prior consent in any form of binding or cover other than that in which it is published and without a similar condition including this condition being imposed on the subsequent purchaser.

This is a work of fiction. Any resemblance to actual persons, living or dead, or actual events is purely coincidental.

Cover image: Illustration 241770920 | Background
© Vladimir Repka | Dreamstime.com

LinguaBooks
Elsie Whiteley Innovation Centre
Hopwood Lane
Halifax HX1 5ER
www.linguabooks.com

*For my family, my friends
present and absent.
This one's for you.*

## About the author

Wayne Martyn is a West Yorkshire born spoken word artist and writer.

He also hosts daytime shows, produces and interviews independent and commercial creative artists, charity spokespeople and an interesting array of guests at community radio station Phoenix FM, where he has been based since 2009.

He is a member of The Halifax Thespians, where he has appeared in pantomimes and assisted with sound, lighting, set design/building and stage management.

Wayne first performed spoken word at Bramsche, Todmorden in 2012. Since then, he has graced stages across the UK, alongside many of his personal heroes, Kit Radford, Nicky Longthorne, Toria Garbutt, Jackie Hagan, ARGH Kid, Thick Richard, Sophie Sparham, Broccan Tyzak-Carlin, Microphone Jack and Robert Steventon to name but a few.

Wayne lives in Halifax, UK.

# Table of Contents

### PART ONE
### My Truth (Citation Needed)

Hello, It's Only Me ................................................................ 12

Aaargh... Zombies! .............................................................. 15

A Nation Of Digital Dummies ............................................. 17

Existence Exists .................................................................... 22

Bad Penicillin ........................................................................ 25

Happestry .............................................................................. 27

Retreat / Retreat ................................................................... 31

Smithereens .......................................................................... 33

Note To Self .......................................................................... 35

Meltdown Paris .................................................................... 37

Miscellaneous Viscera ......................................................... 39

The Vixen .............................................................................. 42

Facial Gymnastics ................................................................ 43

Marshmellow Candycopia .................................................. 47

Love Not Hat (Part 1) .......................................................... 50

Liberate Yourself .................................................................. 54

No Filter Here ....................................................................... 55

Committed Or Not Committed (THAT IS THE QUESTION) . 57

12369 .................................................................. 58
Inter(per)missions / Feeling Of Healing ....................... 60

## PART TWO
### The Movers and the Shakers

Junkie Asylum ........................................................ 64
Prior Convictions ................................................... 66
Vertigo .................................................................. 67
Occam's Razor ...................................................... 68
S & SC .................................................................. 70
Mucky ................................................................... 71
Bibliotech ............................................................. 73
Dodecahedron ...................................................... 74
Semaphore Yelling ............................................... 76
Rap So .................................................................. 77
Colloquialism ....................................................... 79
JHB ....................................................................... 81
Relapsing .............................................................. 83
Knee High, Grasshopper! ..................................... 85
Consequence Of Love .......................................... 86
Song For Kit ......................................................... 88
Clarice Cliffs ........................................................ 90
Vindication Road .................................................. 91

Alienz ................................................................................. 93

BLOOD/ SUGAR/ SEX/ TRAGIK ................................... 96

Submissive Protocol Inc. ................................................ 100

The Only Way Out Is Through ....................................... 102

Quantify Your Expectations (Bus Billboard) .................. 106

Tastes Like Treason ........................................................ 108

Do (Not) Resuscitate ...................................................... 112

Luca ................................................................................ 115

Until Next Time/ RU Not Entertained ........................... 117

# PART ONE

## My Truth
## (Citation Needed)

*Belongings*

## Hello, It's Only Me

Hello, it's only me
An opening gambit, so Lionel Ritchie
I'm not like most poets, sure you'll soon agree
I'm 6ft 4 of pure heartless to the core
I know where the skeletons are buried
Want a finder's fee?

Hello, it's only me
13 minutes late to turn my page on stage
Shaky legs and rafters clinging
Don't wanna dress smart casually
You can stop it with your clicking
It renders me DOA en scene
The external is often semi-palatial
So will you marry me?

Hello, it's only moi
Propping up the bar with "je suis Johnny Guitar"
I'd rather be talking to the trees
Than being given the rulebook nth degree
Your scarily savoir faire face, filling me with anxiety

*Hello, It's Only Me*

Yes, I do like hip hop!

No, I've never seen La Traviata

This isn't the time nor place my friend

To offer me a juice made of lychees and tomata

Hello, it's only me

Solipsist? It's not you, it's … er,

Dancing about like you're the next breakthrough 'thing'

Your words ain't fit enough to advertise a Fisher Price swing

I'm only really half joking, golf witticisms aside

I'm teeing off and aiming the ball at your half-cooked pride

All these years of self promoting

Amount to a lonely existence of fear and foaming

(In Las Nowhere)

Hello, it's only me

The highest home slice pedigree

Feeding on white hot lava, you can stick to your kedgeree

I'm trying to be more healthy at 150kg

My philosophy - excel at staying ground level

*Belongings*

Before the God in you rips your heart out
... and feeds it to the devils
If there's the faintest inkling?
We could be blind
Would you turn the sun up for all time?
It's only me, no royal highness
"Look for the helpers" he wrote...
Come find us...🎤

## Aaargh... Zombies!

We are young. We're depraved.

We are beamed upon this stage

In a zombie parade

Lackadaisical in retrograde.

Chewing on the fat and the marrow of the made.

I used to believe there were monsters hiding behind the couch.

I'd feel the fever hit as the gage raised by disconcerting amounts.

Now we've become the great unwashed. Those dead behind the eyes.

Viscera of victimhood. Bitten by the plagued.

Talking armchair politicians, ourselves by benediction.

Typing out messages like it's a seance for the afflicted.

Ouija creepy. Kinda sleepy. Always weepy. Damsons of distress.

We fight for supposed freedom, but we revel in the mess.

The thick of it, the stress, the countless sleepless nights.

Wishing for a brighter future.

Whilst we're run aground as the rulers run amok.

*Belongings*

The killer blow meets the aftershock.

You know it, don't ya? Humans have failed to recognise

The counterpoint between humanity and evil.

We kill hope as scope for future generations

Is whittled down to a snowflake melting on Satan's pitchforked tongue.

Breathing in through our lungs, bile-ing out through our mouths.

The hatred spewed on message boards. Our karma sent down south.

Below the earth there is a place. A fiery hell or so the occult would like to deceive.

If you're looking for light relief, think NegaPositiv's magnus opus is not for me.

Because the he-said-she-said bullshit performed in the pulpit of liars

Is to control through bullying and stoking pointless fires.

Fuck the conformity of the groupthink. The mask of mob mentality.

You and I know the difference, we are blessed to treat each other with equality.

So the zombies they will rise and we'll chop off their fucking heads.

People like you are the reason people like me are addicted to the meds.

## A Nation Of Digital Dummies

I couldn't give a fuck about your internet friends
How Tommy's getting divorced and Mallory's favourite record is Life Thru A Lens
Your snapchat filters on a plate of chips
Your Instagram post of your pumped-up tits
Everyone these days sees themselves as a social commentator
But I'd rather chew the fat face to face cos I'm a serial masticator

Like this, hate that
Air your dirty laundry so matter of fact
Whatever happened to Tommy?
First friend to many a young teenybopper
Groomer of children or social network copper?
Myspace? Come to my place
Witter on about your favourite kind of cheese
I'd rather take a roundhouse kick to the face
Than swallow any more shitty triviality
This is a public service announcement from NP
Get your head out of your MacBook
And your arse off the settee

*Belongings*

There's a world of wonder out there

It's infinite, no maximum GB (that's gigabytes, yeah?)

Don't you remember the better days?

Kicking footy in the park

But now you're buying virtual chickens

To feed digital seed after dark

Now, it's 2018, hashtags and message sending

Sucked into this matrix- post-modern critique, trending and legitimised loan shark lending

I'd rather converse at my local watering hole

Shake hands, shout nastrovje, chatter boxing freely

Debating the burning issues like 'Mila Kunis or Cat Deeley'


I couldn't give two hoops about your internet friends

Your plenty of fish companion nor your alien lover called Ken

Everyone these days is blogging like it's Hot Potato

But I'd rather get drunk and discuss Nietzsche like a philosophical exacerbator

I am

## A Nation Of Digital Dummies

I find the limitation of characters highlights the
   limitation of your character
Just being honest, that's all, don't mean to sound
   off like I'm mad at ya
See, there's such a thing as too many photos of
   bands on a stage
Because you're not really living in the moment,
   you're living page by page
How much does a hipster weigh? Guess the
   answer's an Instagram
It won't benefit me to see an image of you eating
   toast with jam
Now it's getting perversely silly, the PM wants to
   put restrictions on porn
When he's been fisting the country since the day
   his political career was born
Surfing the web for guns can be misconstrued as
   cyber crime
So I wave my semi-automatic weapon in the
   form of a rhyme

The internet's got a lot to answer for
A soapbox for trolls to whore their wares from
The other day I heard of the bullied girl
Who had her whole life ahead of her
Every reason to live in the world

*Belongings*

She had no escape route at hand to use

So she found relief in the form of a noose

These remorseless illiterate bastards made her life hell

These repugnant molluscs should get back in their shitty shells

The problem as I see it is crystalline clear

Those who abuse freedom of speech should be put to trial

By a jury of our peers who will condemn them with fear

That if you violate the liberty of speech

You should have your mouth sewn shut

Until the end of your years


The purity of paper to pen

Can overpower corrupt bureaucracy

Talking from the heart

Can frequently help us put conflict aside

I'll always attest that demonstrating your opinions

Shall always remain free gratis

But I refute the claim

That those who spout inhumane destruction

Shall always remain free from blame

*A Nation Of Digital Dummies*

I don't care about your internet friends

I only care about my intimate friends

So let's take a vacation from the white and the blue

Before the things you subscribe to override the truths within you

*Belongings*

## Existence Exists

Bad news on a landline

High tides when there's tough times

Dubious movements of the petty crims

Pay at Satan's shady spray tan booth with your seven deadly sins

Lubrications by the hive mind

Can't read shit for all the stop signs

They say a prison is a dwelling of your own doings

One road paved with good intentions

A fork where the other leads you to rack and ruddy ruin


Misanthropes and mitigating circumstances

Light the way like haute couture jack o lanterns

Put your goddamn hands down, don't clap for jinxed anthems

Do the math, they'll be laughing all the way to their mansions


I don't need telling what a swelling of the heart can proximate

*Existence Exists*

The only truism that resonates is to make love to overthrow hate

I don't need it spelling on a billboard two thousand feet high

Because in the end what lives will surely be remembered when it dies


Rogue elements against us, brothers

Sisters, know that we also love you and your covens

Skateboarding through the hoardings of the mourning

Don't piss on my back and tell me it's raining this morning

Dilapidations show off our treatment of these mangers

You want venom? I can hack a miasma of magma for pages and pages and pages

One face is poised and learned; you can read it like scripture

The other appears as a menacing phantom that just feeds off all your lurid addictions


I don't need telling what a swelling of the heart can proximate

The only truism that resonates is to make love overthrow hate

*Belongings*

I don't need it spelling on a billboard two
  thousand feet high
Because in the end what lives will surely be
  remembered when it dies

## Bad Penicillin

Think before you speak
Speak before you think
Either way around society makes it difficult
We evolve in a single blink
We revolve and perpetually move
Towards the good and the bad in humanity
So whoever you are and wherever you're from
I don't mean to lecture, my words mean to stun
You into active pursuit of a future of harmonious living
Where discrimination is flushed out
Bad Penicillin


Talk before you judge
Kneel before you nudge
I'm no religious fanatic
I'm an ordinary man with no brass when shove comes to push
They discuss fucking jargon like group think
I demand you to define such a verbal diarrhoeic stink
Your friends and neighbours in this pretend city are afraid

*Belongings*

To boast of the positive changes and the achievements they've made

We come from a lineage steeped in tragedy and modesty

It's that tried and tested cliché, but a truth nugget all the same

The best things in life are accessible and free

I'm a kamikaze broke poet emotionally and financially

So when I converse with new faces, I feel an overwhelming sense of relief

Knowing we're all in the same ship crashing on the rocks of social disgust

But these are subjects only now we're allowed to truly discuss

Through internet forums, to hell with trolling

We've got enough of them in our ranks, they're the ones for whom we are voting

I hope to assuage you towards good judgement calls and harmonious living

Whereby the good will triumph and evil will rot

Like Bad Penicillin 🎤

## Happestry

A mission statement is all well and good

But is it your mission's work to be drowning the flood?

You've got to search inside, pop under the hood

Before you know it, you'll be dead inside if you don't answer to your best side

That's where the magic happens...


You see I ducked and dived with the demons

My friends were and still are broken down battleships

We all pose for photographs in bars and cinemas

Riot at weekends to forget about our shitty tips

You see I ran with the devil and saw no exit signs

Played canasta with other people's feelings tried to shape the chicanes of their lives

Now as I'm getting older, I'm getting wiser but stupider and slower

We're inundated with trials and tribulations and the need to polish our trophies

We've got to contend in this rigmarole, in this day-to-day charade, higher and lower

The contradictions, the dichotomies, we're all alternatives, adrenaline versus brain freeze

*Belongings*

Hunger to leave a legacy imprinted on the folks we meet along the paths and promenades

But like all living beings we're fucked up complex toys, one minute happy, the next afraid

My aims are fairly simple, mainly true, quite reasonable goals

The world doesn't agree, WE MUST FIT WITHIN BOUNDARIES, BOXES AND ROUND PEG HOLES

I said to my mate Dave the other day that we'd meet up, chill, kick some fictional football arse

Things change, time's in flux, gotta get back to that drawing board, that first term class

We consider the abstractions of nature, over-analyse to distraction

Waylaying moments of hilarious relaxation, of genuine undiluted satisfaction

Because our existence is a mannequin shop model that's forced to be forever redressed

So I think clear that shit up later, it's the weekend, let's unwind our coils to excess

There I go again these days I try and live with a moderation day routine

We're all prescribed with addictive ways to suppress our failures, it's too hard being clean

Let me list 'em

*Happestry*

Prozac, masturbation, fornication, unlimited vodka shots

Television, bad nutrition, crystal meth, cigarettes, pot

Body ideal, touch and feel, being the next John Peel

Bodybuilding, gymnasium gyrating, yoga, Zumba

Justin Bieber, Gaga fever, shitty game shows with Samantha Mumba (exactly, who?)

Meditation, levitation, mass condemnation, discrimination

Nunchucks, tasers, lasers, razors, fire, gas, kettling, marching, demonstration

Good film, bad film, porn film, chick lit

Fast car, big house, bank account, gift card, mobile phone and all that bullshit

Festivals, rituals, sacrifices, being miserable

Cynical, lyrical, satirical, tyrannical, manic, panic, never sitting still

War, famine, pestilence, genocide, apartheid social and spiritual

Judging politicians, presidents, councils, governments, social-work miracles

*Belongings*

These are just a few I ain't got lines and bars to fully complete the collection

There's a million more that can turn you saint to whore upon further inspection

What I'm saying is that with all these flaws we're all kinds of lucky too

On a daily basis it can take the meeting of faces to eradicate all our bleeding art blues

If I think about my authenticity too much, I realise I roam Black Sheep through blurs and phases

Nothing's unique no more; except humanity so we look for an anchor elsewhere

Valuing ourselves is tough turmoil, naked, bare and on the cusp of the tear

I don't have all of the answers, I'm a dancer, chancer, vocal necromancer at the gates of a dystopia we all have to share

But while we're here let's take a minute to dispel troubles and cares

Learn, love, laugh, light and clear the polluted air

Backtrack, remind, reinstate, examine, repair

Tick tock tick tock kick the clock of 21$^{st}$ century injustice

Down the fucking stairs

## Retreat / Retreat

It's said that we only use 10% of our brain's capacity

Well, that's urban myth monolith, internet garbage

Here's my method of thinking

Maybe you do this exact same thing


I smoke cigarettes after dark

Responsibly, not around kids in the park

I put on my fleece step out of the house

Try to keep my parents in slumber, quiet ninja mouse

Pull a cancer stick from its warm sheath

Ignoring the health warnings underneath

Light the tip and take that first huge exhale of oxygen

Purse my lips, count slowly in my head, never get to ten

All the day's troubles and adversities are Pandora-proofed

Trapped in my brainbox, now I begin to feel loose and aloof

Questions without answers, so far, arrive like pre-empted waves

*Belongings*

Things like "would I look good with a beard" and "what ever happened to nu rave?"

I feel energized, revitalised and ready to go back in my Batcave

Type another fucking angry e-mail to the webpage of the Daily fucking Mail

I'm not suggesting take up smoking, it's a filthy vice

Tobacco scent clings to your clothes and breath, where's the chewing gum and Old Spice when you need it

What I'm saying is take those seldom minutes of relief and use them like Black and Decker tools

To drill into the mayhem and enjoy the resulting pools of cool

I smoke cigarettes after dark

I don't deserve a medal for this pearl of wisdom, go on then. Just a house mark.

Retreat / retreat. What's good for me isn't always good for thee.

## Smithereens

In this canyon of great noise

We immerse ourselves in each other

Sit back and watch the world (erupt into smithereens)

Knowing we were just a temporal anomaly

Screen blips, fragmented, fractured, fucked

From the get-go we went against the grain

Searching for belonging, finding it, then running opposite directions

This yearning light, deep, bright and building

Ready to fall into the ether, love and lust combined

To make a rapture that has only been written about

Secretly in books never read by the human eye

This beautiful endeavour travelled together under stormy skies

Oceanic and singular to the light

In this corrosive ballast poised

We declare all non-sequiturs unbounded

Stand up and capture the moment (careen into smithereens)

Heightened by the shape and form of nothingness

*Belongings*

Treen bits, segregates, satiated, supped up

All that lets go yielded and redux

In this canyon of great noise

Sit back and watch the world (cascade into smithereens)

Syncopated blast beats that shudder through the valley of boneyards

This dystopian voice arches through my ears

Singing "Whatever this is. Whatever this means"

This plasticine world comes unready and far less poised

Than the void that allows us to burst at the seams

Tragic timing, but somehow emerging like bittersweet comedy

This canyon of great noise

Thrown into the sea (forever to be smithereens)

A celestial atrocity

## Note To Self

It's just a note to self
Been dreaming of disappearing stealth
In the black room, developing negatives
There's a tiny little bottle of soul sedatives
You can pass the buck all you like
There's no freewheeling on this motorbike

It's just a note to self
So alluring when it's on the shelf
Idolise the pretty things, positive posturings
Naval gazing at the belly button etchings
You can get it at half the usual price
Nothing sweeter than a bit of avarice

It's just a note to self
I suppose that it has passed the twelfth
Nights drag on like a fuzzy omnibus
Smoking Gauloises till it's burnt to rust
Shooting stars out of a barricade
It's easy once you know you're being played

*Belongings*

3:13 am
Internal scene
It hurts you and me
Internally, eternally
3.14 am
On the couch
Lounging lizard
Pinned on a 'note to self'

## Meltdown Paris

From French Quebec to Guadeloupe
I see beauty, they speak true
Together through fight and passion
Love and unity, height of fashion
Architects past and futures
Notre Dame, Parc des Princes, Latin Quart
I'm overwhelmed and overjoyed
In Parisian air, I'll find myself
Beyond the pollution and political climate
Lies a beating lionheart in the city of romance
Lovers and lusters in their night-time dance acts
Brothers and sisters marching on as one
Bon soir, mon ami, I hear from strangers
The kindness, the soul food in MBK, down Gare du Nord
I'm humbled by kindred spirits, no separations
(Unless you're counting mother tongues)
This is a country waving a flag worth fighting for
D'accord monsieur
New York dilettante outside the hotel lobby
We share a cigarillo to pass through translation
Says "here on business or vacation"

*Belongings*

My response "just to get away"

She offers me a trip to the Hamptons in Summer

But I say "can't chat, even though I'd love to stay"

Can't sleep in the sheer beauty of this wondrous place

A sense of belonging I always hoped existed in this sprawling metropolis

Boldness of the natives, loud voices, marching placard

Hustlers, vagabonds, bohemians, out-of-towners, travellers

All in a weird harmonic ecosystem

I love Paris with all my heart cuz to the beat I've started to listen

But I'm drinking too much and the waiters can tell

I'm argumentative as fuck with my company and beginning to yell

What a place to have a meltdown in Gay Paris

Turns out I'm just struggling to start anew back home, you see

When I arrive in England again, I tune in to a brand new me

It was all because of that amazing, humbling, beauteous city 🎙

## Miscellaneous Viscera

Smile as if we're in passion with painful strokes

A mural of the ages, let's pleasantly coast

Whilst coaxing out a hoax on a plateau made for two

Sync or swim, it's your grin, amour is armour and it's Lucy I choose

Loosely based on a 60's paperback, pulped fiction

Totally faded, all its sparkle darkened in an almanac for addictions

Waylaid heavy hearts down a terracotta snicket

Stamps on our non-conformity, twisted tongues can lick it.

Razor-blade sashays along my eyebrow

If it tickles, we'll be the trickle-down fields where we once submitted our vow

To take on the world together even when it wouldn't allow

You were always on my mind, each past and present future, why, when, how

The cigar scented lollipop you thrashed against my gums

You took the wrong route to Muscle Beach, babe, cos I didn't have the guns

*Belongings*

Fond remembrance, a cascading semblance of an ill-fated date by a blizzard forest

Allowed for lips and hips to slacken, predilections flow more honest

You marked my skin in red henna ink with a sentence that felt like a lifetime's confession

"If kismet's wind threw us together, love is 9 tenths of the law, and you are now under my possession"

My nose began to bleed, a cobalt-coloured projection of miscellaneous viscera


Did I ever swallow the skeleton key named courage, face up and reply?

"I will die for my art but not in vain but just so they know I'm a part time purveyor of semi fictitious literature..."

I warned you in lines five and six

Be aware that I live between your ears and most days I'm just here to parlour trick you with premium content and ventilative wit.

The faux tattoo began to appear as a contusion on my wrist

So I quickly scribed a diatribe in the form of my teenage year Top 10 chart topping lists

The pen took remote control, a mitten militia

*Miscellaneous Viscera*

You promised scorched earth and delivered nuclear fission

Slew me like dragon-fire, me the man without roots (for at least a while)

Sucker-punched in the kisser

The knives will always be out because our affections are missiles

Vanished from the everlasting, brought pure by these kisses

To this day when I think of you my nose still bleeds

Invisible

Miscellaneous

Viscera

*Belongings*

## The Vixen

This year taught me not to trust my self
The flicks and tricks of the Black Dog
Took apart my mental health
But then you appeared, all shiny and renewing
I'd forgotten the mind-numbing words I'd been eschewing
You are the Vixen, my TLM
From the coffee shop to the tunnel by the ATM
Limonada and caffeine reminiscence
All I long for and all we treasure
Me in a T-shirt, below the jacket of leather
You with that scent like strawberries and heather
We converse and remunerate like they do in the black and whites
Our kinship clandestine but watertight
I love you through the darkest days
You message me through the dangerous nights
The Vixen, she's my everything

## Facial Gymnastics

Copycat plagiarists
With little time for little old atheist me
Go and pour yourself a cup of nettle tea
You self-aggrandizing sexless swine
Fog on the Tyne, three pronged forks that fail to shine
Accosted me outside of Costa
Said you'd make me a superstar
I bet it's fun driving yer daddy's Jaguar
Moaning about the extent of LinkedIn portfolios
You're morally remortgaged and it fucking shows
Do you sit outside when the snow comes down?
Wishing chalk wasn't chang up your dirty snout.
Lyrical boom boxer, WM
A garter in your larder, ready to take your femme.
I mean it, the woman you deceived to be the blushing bride.
Told me that loving you was like a rerun of Homicide

*Belongings*

1,2,3, still too many trap clappers
Not enough emcees without phoney degrees
1,2,3 still too many fake Chuzzlewits
On your BBC Threes
1,2,3 I wanna take you pastures new and slap you wet fish silly
1,2,3 this ain't a pissing contest so put away your…

Playbook for the masochists
I'm eschewing many pacifists
By hanging out with actresses
Swell, these feelings so imaginative
Facial gymnastics
Relapsing on caffeine and blastocysts
Facial gymnastics
The Slugger is the baddest there is…

Used to pull cunning stunts with Mike & Ollie
Outside the HTC till it was sundown
Now I'm paying out on the doubters
With the smokey tears of a clown
Here's the Money Shot, I don't give a jot
In your binder, just a casual reminder

*Facial Gymnastics*

That I'm flyer than Concord

I rip out sucker MC's vocal cords

Tie them to a sidewinder

There's no F in phenomenal

But there's two in effigy

I'm settling kindling on your corpse

Like "say it don't spray it"

With your irreverential demonocracy

It's plainer than Doris Day

In the back of an UBER

NegaPositiv will outlive the mushroom cloud of Brexitgeddon

Slugger is about to jump your beatmatching bones like a puma

You want the whole enchilada?

As promised on its packaging?

Whose line is it anyway?

You see me wearing a wedding ring (nada)

I like spaghetti bolognese, beach walks

And Martin Scorsese movies

361369 give me a call if you're feeling groovy

*Belongings*

I'm eschewing many pacifists
By hanging out with actresses
Swell, these feelings so imaginative
Facial gymnastics
Relapsing on caffeine and blastocysts
Facial gymnastics
Slugger is the baddest there is…
Facial gymnastics
It's my birthday, I'm lavishing
Facial gymnastics
So throw in the towel unless you're ravishing

## Marshmellow Candycopia

Trying to salvage something meaningful from my mind like I'm an apothecary

The twists and turns and stomach churns light the litmus for the future is very scary

If only we could sit atop a treehouse with bird's-eye view receptions

Looking down onto the world that's become tormented by deceptions

Upon closer detail, we're just fodder for the disenfranchised demagogues

You can't make a real fire unless you burn some fucking logs

I'll sleep under a starry canvas, Tog 24, beside the marshmellowed candycopia you call solitude

Pardon me for being so rude, but if love really tarnishes the inkwell isn't hate what needs to be removed?

"Nice chatting with you on this winter's day," my spirit guide retorts

I'm spinning the wheel of chance like it's a bridal dance and my cummerbund is caught

On the fruitless effigies of my past and present take on a somnambulist sequestered surveillance

*Belongings*

We're on the frontline of fuck-all unless we're using our tasers

To enact a war against elitism, Negapositiv versus The Grind Downers

Linguistically we're all subjugated and lyrically we're out-of-towners

When we don't see a reflection of ourselves in the coven that surrounds

I'd rather die poor and kiting than dick about rich and be stuck in the middle ground

This isn't like the time I tried to summon a hex

On those who aren't fans of Cigarettes After Sex

I understand your music choices are yours to cherish

We're all sonic mnemonics born to stream as we kick back and watch industries perish

And what's with the abbreviation of companies with sickening ideologies

Pogoing their logos through our eye sockets as if it'll benefit us biologically

I stand with those fighting to better the cause, no slogans in my cereal

But I ain't a perfect citizen, I'll still emish my carbohydrates in a way that's immaterial

The underbelly is seedy because it's just above from where we cum, shit and piss

*Marshmellow Candycopia*

If you think that's crude, wait until I spit a dirty sequel to my debut produced by The Actionist

There's an expiry date on my raving rants, better increase the size of my internal mortgage

Cos the house that the previous occupants built is upon a burial ground set adrift on detritus, a so-called posher word for garbage, pish

Trust me and cash me outside cos I don't know where I'm going with this Wilhelm Scream of conscious uncoupling couplets

Roll it out to the public before you've finished praising your muses and subjects, cuz

I'm trying to stay humble in this topsy turvy apple-crumble hipster economy

Pass me the scissors and scalpel, my own worst enemy needs a frontal lobotomy

What even is life without comic relief, chief?

So grab your Mills & Boon pseudo philosophy and hand me over to sleep.

*Belongings*

## Love Not Hat (Part 1)

Advantageous can be outrageous

A thing to say in Brexitgeddon ages

Who hates the poor? Who feeds the rich?

Guilt-free secateurs worn by raconteurs on the pitch

What does it even mean with your subliminal meme?

Tame the evidential provincial state of unawares at its seams

Diabolic the diatribes amongst the ditches

Brass knuckle sandwiches and a penchant for tattoos that read:

"BITCHIN"


LOVE NOT HAT


Here to spread a message of love not hat

I wore the self-aggrandizing twat badge like a strangling cravat

Now I love myself and that scares you too

Talking to my inner monologue

The silent elephant in the room

What was once a daily grind

*Love Not Hat (Part 1)*

All the fears superseded the appetites
Unleashed upon a stage
Perfect by design
Cathartic and far from refined.
(Three sugars and a steel spine)

LOVE NOT HAT

CITY:
Saw a homeless man the other day
Bought him a bottle of water, left it at his feet
A woman walked my way
Tutted and sniggered as if he didn't deserve a little money
They're putting spikes in trolley shelters
When they could be supporting those who need shelter
The press gang say, "these fuckers are panhandling scum"
My response: How would you feel if it was your dad, mom, daughter or your son?

*Belongings*

TOWN:

I see buskers drop their hats

I hear their stories as I pass

There's love and pain in their songs

Where so easily there could lie hate

I supposed it depends on how the streets are paved

Call it preachy but the message shalt always be

LOVE NOT HAT

No matter where the compass settles

I'm the diplomatic acrobat

Cos that fuzzy emoting when your schadenfreude ain't promoting

We all scream for ice cream dreams

But some melt down on the laundry mat

When the welcome sign is covered in excrement

Off the bat, I wanna tell you that it's plain to see

That we've all sucker-punched virtual reality

Love Island makes us homicidal

The term 'beach ready' pressurizes us into hiding

Call it a missing ringlet on a severed finger

*Love Not Hat (Part 1)*

I wouldn't take an E from a man who looks like
   Jerry Springer


LOVE NOT HAT


LOVE NOT HAT


Through megaphone and thinking cap

*Belongings*

## Liberate Yourself

I coulda been a contender

But the odds were fixed (the jig is up) and the horse returned to sender

Liberate yourself, at least for your own amusement

Freedom came Saran-wrapped, it couldn't breathe new life into this first refusal

So non-committal in affairs of the beating heart

I was a husky busker on the streets of love misfiring poisoned darts

Most desires waxed and waned, lust played me like a piano

I've been searching for the 'supposed one' but they will never match up

To my poster girl adoration of Meadow Soprano

## No Filter Here

Pay lip service to snakes
Just watch it all unfold as earth quakes
Beneath the stair-rods of hate
That inert feeling leaves shame
No filter here, my dear
Less than zero fucks given, it's crystalline clear
We don't do fear round our way
Got a better plateau of words to spray
The sprawling metropolis stinks of piss and bile
You've outrun the menacing menial mile
Reptiles stacking odds
To replace humans with robots
Is just a hysterically unjust disease
Begging and pleading like a mouse after cheese
Like paper tigers reeling in for the long night kiss
We resist the discontentment, it's a swing and a miracle miss
Sealed avengence, stolen lust abandon
Moet for the Poets, what's left is an omnipotent shambles
Realign your fever dreams, place them on a countertop

*Belongings*

Burst the idols at the seams and for God's sake crop the shot

It's a million to one under a burning inhumane sky

The hive mind may whisper in your ear, but it doesn't decide when you die

It's a foolish errand, in itself an Irish goodbye

You're driving a lemon into the world's biggest lie

That there's a filter here, let's not get it twisted, there's no humble pie

## Committed Or Not Committed
(THAT IS THE QUESTION)

We seldom speak these days
It's as if your silence contextualizes the pain I feel
Looking to free my synapses, a runaway train
Maybe better apart but coming together we'd heal
It's at the altar of you
Where I find it best to kneel
But that's dangerous
I've lived my life on an uneven keel
Maybe it's deep rooted in my genetic make up
Can't stomach the idea of a breakup
God my head just needs a shake up
Fucking hell I need to wake up
From this ideological reverie of perfect love
It doesn't exist inside a steel glove
It's more of a snow globe broken in two
Somehow the snow magnifies the coldness of youth
Yes, I'm trying to be less uncouth
Forsooth, damaged another tooth
Chewing on a pen-lid as I scribe
You another unrequited electronic lullaby

*Belongings*

## 12369

I'm off to pastures new
How about you?
12369
24852
Dragging your feet across the floor
A bodice ripper and more
Can't find it in oneself to self-adore
Just time after time scrambling for the cord
It's coercive, it's corrosive, it's touch-paper blues
All melting inside the pot to make a rotten stew
Dare angels tread on this tormented terrain
Leave a final note as your body bleeds into the frame
Posing mannequin-ish, this child play
Smoke my life's work into the ashtray
I'm back from pastures new
How are you doing mate?
12369
An altered fugue state
We've got a lot of numbers in the rolodex
Smash the system into pieces of Perspex

*12369*

Initiative hanging out at the mini bar
Close but no bastard cigar
Dancing after dinner is a must
To leave the past discrepancies concussed
It's a column with a plus
Now wouldn't that taste lush?

*Belongings*

## Inter(per)missions / Feeling Of Healing

Ladies and gentlemen, here's a public service announcement
About the size of my endowment
Erecting bliss into the cosmos
Misery is as misery does at its upmost
You've all got your raffle tickets?
Bing bing bing the winner is...
Fences were invented for pickets
So fuck these inter(per)missions
The interval is a farcical charade
There is no relaxation readymade
(Let's put the world on pause, that ain't a thing, of course)
We're only atoms dressed to the nine of spades
In the hopes of tonight getting laid
So take your seats, the second act is about to begin
Didn't they read you the riot act on your way back in?
Overt your eyes for a second, I'm the humble narrator
"Ears avow, oh my stars!" come sarcastic commentators

*Inter(per)missions / Feeling Of Healing*

The truest thing I ever said on record
Is that love is a losing sport
The curtain raises and the players are all gone
Because begs the question
Do I, do I, belong???

# PART TWO

The Movers and
the Shakers

*Belongings*

# Junkie Asylum

What was once coined the funny farm

My home for a spring of mental arithmetic that doesn't correlate

Years after the depression and decadent obscenery

Smoked way too much green and drank way too much mind bleach

(I recommend it only for the strong minded and weak willed)

They welcomed me at the entrance

I was en a trance

(Geddit?)

Dancing through the corridors with twisted jubilation

That my existence had boiled down to this incarceration

Well, well, it's a junkie asylum

A term I came up with on the sly

I felt like CCTV had won a prize and it was my shadow

Poisoned with an arrow of injustice, Bruce Fucking Wayne

With no manners, a play on words that kinda stammers

*Junkie Asylum*

The green one, the red one, the white
All getting me higher than a kite
Take twice and add regular blood tests
The men in lab coats will come and get me at breakfast
Paranoid pursuits, Polaroid snapshots
Of a time when I'd endeavoured to lose all reason and narrative plot
This man-child forgotten by his own beliefs
In manic happiness, all at once beset by grief
There were 'characters' in these walls, some standing only a few feet tall
All hooked on designer drugs and cuisine therapy
That was the kicker that got me substituting pain for apathy
Lethargic in a tragic kingdom with kindling ablaze
Couldn't be bought or sold as just a phase
I stumbled into a maze; labyrinth life suited me to a tee
Until one bloke escorted his fist to my nose for a bloody fee
Life in 4K, no bonhomie
The 'junkie asylum' gates are now behind me

*Belongings*

## Prior Convictions

Jumped the fence at 8 am
Couldn't find a way to stem
The blood flow from my seeping hand
The only way we reprimand
Prior convictions I used to possess
Like the only way of living is to revel in the mess
Dynamite personalities clashing on cue
I felt so much Euphoria as in the story of Rue

I've become expert at spotting bad signs
Never coming in with first prize
Still frames bathed by neon lights
All of my assumptions were outright lies

## Vertigo

Questioning all I survey from this height
Hollering into a mic since I was a little tyke
The stage is set and the show is everything we know
Basking in an altered reality of ego
In my mind there's an initiation, strike one
Forgotten how to harness all the joy in fun
Said my sayonarras with a smoking gun
Enter the swagger, this is how to stun

*Belongings*

## Occam's Razor

Attached to my brain, there's a taser
How did it get there?
Occam's razor
Pull a rabbit from a hat
It's a trick of the ages
How did it get there?
Occam's razor

I lost self-esteem, just didn't love living
Every numbing heartbeat left me a battered cynic
There was too much dust to wonder
Too many to rust and plunder
All I could hear was a buzzing noise in the head
Like lightning and tropical thunder
Electric sparks connecting to nothingness
Joy waves synced to an out-of-date disk drive marked "emptiness"
I'm half drunk, half eaten, no redemption left to seek
The outer shell representing something uniquely antique

*Occam's Razor*

Tarred and feathered by the pleasure brush
It's enough to make an idiot cherry-picker
  coloured blush

*Belongings*

## S & SC

Sweet and sour chicken for two
Self-proclaimed geekdom
A bit of Grand Theft Auto then it's beddy-byes
Sizing up a king size tree
Smoke till I'm aloof and leafy
Beached and broken never scattered
Somewhat scarred by the noughties
They fucked me up for the reasons given
In my portfolio of words and verses rendered
"Return to a sender who no longer exists in such a format"

Don't want to be sofa surfing when I'm 44
Don't want to be knocking at hesitation's door
Don't want a clean amputation of the cutting floor
Don't want the redemption that comes with giving up scores

## Mucky

There's a perverted stance, a tribal dance, salute the cuticles
They grind and grin in polished high rises, sweaty cubicles
Jousting for freedoms that they can't afford
I won't speak for them but I'll stand up for them, so they won't be ignored


The slander, slut-shaming supposed shaman pose a true threat
Their dirty laundry aired for skin that's bared, you place your bets
Against the love that goes unfulfilled, the days that torture continues
There's no amusement park party as they turn their screws


I knew a girl called Tequila Mockingbird or at least her pseudonym was
She died by the square when no one was around to cause a fuss

*Belongings*

The brutality, inhumanity, she suffered on the reg
   is now over
But her life was far more precious than the car
   that broke her body into clovers

Life comes with no trigger warning
Do your best and quit the fawning
Sex is a weapon at times used against the
   beautiful ones
Sex is a tragic ending when used against the
   beautiful ones

## Bibliotech

I write and scribe these diatribes

Break out in hives and give high fives

Tremendous endless friendless sentences

Do their best to correlate their penances

5 and 20 pence and restlessness

Chalked upon a bored board aboard a horde of denizens

The bibliotech is peaking and I'm reaching for the pen

Because the sword that cut my umbilical cord is in a case of emotions that existed only then

An atlas of cloud formations linking up to the fascinations

Of all the hills I roamed and paths I strolled in search of adoration

Calculating undulations at the shitty petrol stations

There are faces attached to voices that breath idle penetrations

The bibliotech is a swathing babe that renders crying like a dilettante

My biggest worry today is whether I can weather this sans italic font

*Belongings*

## Dodecahedron

The impending tragedy is burgeoning faster
Whilst I change the channels as I put away my pasta
There seems to be ten sides to every story
Encroached by the rapture, bedazzled in gory
I tried to hide my disconcerted face
I wrapped it up with ill determinant faith
The fingers grasp at straw shaped effigies
Hostages of loving yourself and your worst enemies
There seems to be ten sides to every story
It's a play time thing, so Jackanory
Quantifiable as a sandcastle in a monsoon
As reliable as your most favoured cartoon
The antagonist and the protagonist walking side by sidewinder
Acting up for the cameras, the daily reminder
Neighbourhoods watch on with scarce commentary
The villainy is remiss as it's your own territory

*Dodecahedron*

There is more than a dodecahedron working the angles

Heaven and hell collide through the fevered mangle

*Belongings*

## Semaphore Yelling

When the woe beside me tied me up in knots

The wolves came knocking holding flags to their chests

Happiness appeared as a farang, a concept at odds

With all I knew, alluring and turquoise at the bruise

Then there was you, a tall glass of milky dreaminess

A jolt to the system, passionate with pistons cocked

You were like a walking magazine cover of blissful aptitude

But as it turns on a wheel, life made us question everything

Taking liberties in the inventory of love

Now I can't stomach the fact I let you see me down

The dystopian cocktail like it was a running joke

Enjoy what's round the bends, friends can be partner-shaped too

With semaphore yelling and the swelling inauguration

Of the darkness imbued by two, it's on one hand a picnic

The other a magnificent ruse

# Rap So

Mad losses, enhancement advancement shall recoup

Pavement presence of the Blue Man Group

Let's elope, have six summers, be basking in the fruit

Rap so, clap-trap calypso, sat in economy seat 82

He's a dead ringer for Hugh Jackman she said

As she watered the pachyderms and ate some garlicky bread

Terminology like 'on fleek' went out with the double denim

Over jazzy interludes, too many semibreves and minims

Clever Cedric compartmentalising car parts in the cedar avenue

I'm on my new hook now, it's a jam, it's a 5-star rebuke review

Dreaming of way back, hospital admission, on a morphine drip

He belonged to angels rather than demons, but never let the mask slip

Friends all lined up like a firing squad, beach bods in entropy

The bees buzzing cousins all work in dentistry, toothache soliloquy

*Belongings*

Dandelion minds chasing ribbons down the motorways

Tastebuds craving a concoction of Hennessey and cranberry Ocean Spray

Deviant crosswords at crossroads licking the rusty side of the coin

He ain't ever threshold the halls, he contemplated uprooting to Des Moines

The radio's on an axis spinning funk-o-tronic bangers that slam dunk

Alleviating the mantle core of the mattress of the dead-beat poet punk

Mandolins rouse the half woke, toking on the school playing field

The antidote to microphone nerves is to have a subject you can yield

Let's revoke the past indiscretions, seething got us nowhere but juvenile

Play that lyric for a high point ratio, scrabbling with the tiles

I am ready for the next chapter, et voila, it's the prestige we admonished

That's the Judas kiss and kismet wish, a perfect dilated diluted tonic

Johnny Guitar found his backbone, it was in the ladies' spotless manicured nails

The future is whatever we make it and there's no need to top and tails

## Colloquialism

Her mind is extravagantly expressive

My toothpaste kisses empathise with the walls of her mouth

If less is truly more, I'm a whore with trinkets, so genial but depressive

Words as prophesy, can't get the colloquialisms out

Rage us into submission, I'll be your lap dog, pontificating

They lined up and gave us 7 days, called it an extended vacation in vacating

The friend zone is a horseshit concoction made up by trash TV

I hate the thought of you crossing the Rhine and drinking iced tea without me

No menace attached, I'm the salubrious butler here

Bringing you the new sensations of a bona-fide shutdown year

I'm yearning, ears burning, hoping for your wanton messages of lust

All I get is the tumbleweed treatment in the kingdom for the concussed

*Belongings*

It's as if you've predictively texted me to say, "that's all folks!"

Like acme with acne, I've become a fool to roast

Her mind saunters around the room looking for drama

What's worse is that she's hooked up to a chemically-induced Dharma

## JHB

Just hunt bliss
It's all I wish
To be a motherfucking motormouth
A prize fighter
The best in the biz
I don't desire more than is at hand
You can come with me to the wonderland

Just hunt bliss
Connect my fist
Into a mammoth appetiser
The new Kaiser
Is the greatest living nothing
Boys and girls
Listen to this
The greatest hit maker
Macabre debonair dish

Just hunt bliss
The reason we co-exist
In an egocentric circus

*Belongings*

Devoid of loving purpose
I am on fire with being adjacent to
The God in me is the God in you
Tao Blitz
I wouldn't trade half a day
Just to be knee deep in paradise piss
For once and for all
Just hunt
Just hunt
Just hunt bliss

# Relapsing

I want to drink until the fountains dry
I want to snort the mountains, inject the sky
I want to cut my skin off and wear a new sheath
I want to bury my head in the underneath
I want to collapse into your aching arms
I want to fairy dust sprinkle the lucky charms
I want to go where no man has ever dared before
I want to ingest a pride of lions and an ambush of tigers
I want to desecrate another dreamless sleep
I want to raise my hours and countless sheep
I want to relapse when the earth looks still
I want to apologise to those who's joys I kill
I want to sacrifice my body to a higher power
I want to eat French cheeses by the Eiffel Tower
I want to give up and give in and give out and give light
I want to learn what's wrong with always wanting to be right
I want to caress your hair as you whisper Giovanni's Room
I want to kneel at the temple of your womb
I want to smell fresh cut flowers every morning

*Belongings*

I want to give you a smile with no need for trigger warnings

I want to smoke away the days in unbridled ecstasy

I want to free myself from what's been taking hostage of thee

## Knee High, Grasshopper!

The machines are out to control us

Contraptions of ever enduring mankind gone wild

I don't feel the need to be a reflector

A spokesperson for a timeline that refuses to shine

Knee-high socks on a grasshopper, that's graphic

Fatalistic at least by design

You've lost that anatomic feeling

Pseudonym tsunamis of a tragic kind

What burns is the burgeoning token-ist approach

No wonder they cancel to appease

Knee high socks on a grasshopper, that's tantamount to phantasm

Housing prices go soaring for the rat race in chasm

*Belongings*

## Consequence Of Love

You don't seem to be descending into repression

The latest trends don't phase you, I like that, it's refreshing

Words like 'enough' and 'fragility' won't appear in your vocab

I reached out for your love, consequence of not paying the bar tab


We listened to Disintegration in amazed silence

I shielded us from the world and its violence

Feelings sentimentally provoking the lustre, sapphires that shine

I impeached our love, consequence of never knowing the sketch was mine


35 years have passed and the hourglass offers a glimmer of futures ripe

35 years have passed and the hallway paintings show my art is of dramatic type

35 years have passed and our families are older but bolder in every way

35 years have passed but there's still lipstick on the Camels you smoke left in the ashtray

*Consequence Of Love*

If one day, the jig was up, buttercup, cinematic climbs await

I don't subscribe to an idiom of enchanted fortune and fame

If one day, the curtain falls and we fall into an audience with baited breath

I won't be aware what's right though I'm sure I'll harness every screed that's left

Of this

Consequence of love

Looking down on us

*Belongings*

## Song For Kit

You are the essence of being. (We are we collectively but we are also more than ever, I, that is the key.) The joy in your eyes is waning but I'm lighting a candle for you to see. (Don't let your voice be caught in the winds of others' destructive ways). We are ether, we are oblivion, we are tied to everything and nothing at all. Equally blessed and cursed. Born from the ground and laid to rest in the Earth. But we are so much more than just food for the worms. Each speck of stardust we are made from, each cell divides and unites (the convex and concave, the afraid and the brave). I love the truth and hope you represent. I wouldn't Trade it, I'm in your Club, since we met. SB read about love life and life will love you (always resonated) Through the ecstasy of real happy, to the soul-crushing pain. The sky is never really blue. It's a complex hue. Clouds will pass and rain will follow. Skin, vessels, bones and a head full of sorrow. It's like an asteroid hit and my ashtray heart is now hollow. But I will never forget the moments shared, the embraces over distance and the connection we made. I'm agnostic but I'm closer to something than ever before, out of my apathy, edging out of the shade. You hit me like a tornado with a smile and a stillness, like calming arms around my mind. You will never know how much, but you are one of a kind. Whatever happens next, there's no severing the bond.

*Song For Kit*

Because she touched a part of me with gentle, warming words like hands and I whisper in her ear, "blackbird, thank you for making me know what it is to belong."

*Belongings*

## Clarice Cliffs

When the temptress of the precipice comes knocking

Go to University and fight all your adversities

I took the Clarice Cliffs with a spliff and 3-inch quiff

We loved Alan, he kept us safe, a motley band of misfits

Heartbreaker Sal, Rapscallious Raz, Screwball Si

To name but a feweth, my best mate Dave years after

(I spy, with my little eye, a miscreant from another mother)

## Vindication Road

I fell in love down Vindication Road

The streets were lined with trumpeters

I fell apart down Vindication Road

The roads flooded with the blood of the puppeteers

I fell asleep in Vindication Road

The traffic lights woke me up

I fell asleep in Vindication Road

Said that already cos I wrote the book


On being an underrated, over-hated

Placid guy with a kinder nature

Carbon dated, middle class stature

Cryogenically frozen and awoken to up and ta-dah!

Have a happy heart attack, you crazy bastards!

On being a bad dad joke teller

Fart smeller, Old Yeller in a tea cosy

On being a man of many talents

But none of them was love

I missed the gauntlet

When shove came to push

*Belongings*

I graduated from Vindication Road

Left the lunacy behind me from that postcode

I matriculated Vindication Road

My intentions were cruel, call me Sarah Michelle Gellar in a suit

I employed the dustmen on Vindication Road

Gave me a ripened sense of self worth

I burned like a matchstick on Vindication Road

Cos the cigarettes were put out like the binbags and the taxis


On this avenue of possibilities

The sequential irreverential deities

My vision askew I fell through the cracks

As the pavement relaxed at 23 degrees fuck all

The allure beats the cure

The allure beats the cure

What are we staying here for?

When the doors are all shut

On Vindication Road

And the last order bell rings no more

## Alienz

Tobacco smoke lights a beacon as I beat the pathways home

The chaos of the skies acts as an assurance that we're not alone

I don't fall for conspiracies, these idle brains are fit to burst

Only concerned by the inert feeling that we're treading someone else's earth

Centuries and millennia of space debris supposedly combined

To build our houses, trees, beaches and seas, would a Big Bang have so aligned?

A trillion and more miraculous molecules make a single bead of my flop sweat

Every Sunday the religious horde pray for mercies like they're in a deity's debt

I'm told that Doomsday beckons, though we are alive death surrounds us

So, we venture to bars hoping we'll single out a partner to quell the ornery fuzz

If money is at evil's root, so glad I'm bleeding dollar broke

Thereby kindness seems like pure honey if it's used to soothe and not to choke

*Belongings*

The best view of heaven is always gonna be from hell

But the sinister ministers amongst us haven't got a soul to sell

Politicking swine tanned Tango and the so-called intelligentsia of Bullingdon Boys Club

They don't wanna mess with the devil cos they know he'll fuck 'em up

These are the things floating around my noggin when it's 3 am and I'm scared to sleep

Look out my bedroom window to see weird flying saucers whilst trying counting sheep

See, as far as I can make out, there must be some sort of other life existing

This may just be a mirage, a hologram, level 23 on a game we're all resisting

(To lose at.)

There's good and evil, right and wrong, but this planet doesn't balance the scales

I believe in aliens because humanity has, well, kinda epic failed.

Spoke to God in a phone box if you recall my previous religion fuelled dalliance.

But my head got too fucking noisy with his altruistic but one-sided stance.

Falling in and out with reason, ask the Internet.

*Alienz*

Like backing a horse that's good for glue, now place your bets.

There's people, actual real people, twittering and redditing about the earth being flat and hollow.

I know if I'm looking for a cause to cling onto, they're surely not the ones to follow

(Friend request delete)

There's kids with guns, nuns with nunchucks

I know I'm being exaggeratory but when it comes to truth, looks like we give no fucks

The world news views injected into our eyeballs 'n earlobes

Tabloids trash talking, it's as if being educated by the news acts like a sanity probe.

We are invested to be tested, suppressed by lies and fear.

Maybe Nostradamus was onto something, this universe isn't primed for Armageddon though we're somewhere near.

At the same time, you probably think I'm mad, that my common-sense ship has set sail.

But damn it, I believe in aliens cos it's pretty obvious humanity's off the rails.

*Belongings*

## BLOOD/ SUGAR/ SEX/ TRAGIK

What's a little cash transaction between lovers - nothing

The spill of crimson between lovers after the fact - it means everything

He lied, he controlled, he contrived, he stole, he piggybacked on her misery

Blood sugar sugar blood sugar sugar blood blood

V1.

Tommy stitched a yarn of fable's faith

He was well aware of the dangerous approach of the lecherous snakes

Sold a baggy outside the Towers at a quarter to three

Proposed to Mischa in his finest attire outside HMV

Tommy's just like me, modest man mountain, a dapper squire

He had first-world problems, like pissing in plastic bottles and then setting them on fire

He's not a pyromaniac, he's a hypochondriac

Lived his life on the move, down the bad seed side of the tracks

No one ever told T that a broken aortic pump never mends

## BLOOD/ SUGAR/ SEX/ TRAGIK

He stood and puffed out his chest and stubbed the cigarette out on his camera lens

Because the movie on his eyelids told the story of a boy with learning difficulties

From panic attacks in bus stations, he couldn't relax, he couldn't breathe, a trick with no sleeve

Rude awakening one velvet morning, awoke the suppressed beast within

Took a shiv in one hand and inscribed onto his petrified skin

"An eye for an eye, a tooth for a tooth"- these words of wisdom somehow now became taboo

The clues in the name, it's Tommy - like a pinball wizard he fled

Into the night to meet Mischa beneath the tree where they first met

He never made it past the snicket, a company of wolves marked out their threat

In the blink of a firefly minute, game over, there lies his carcass by the canal, he and his fiancée would cease to be wed

Chorus

V2.

The piece of the plot that you're missing, a jigsaw hole in the grand design

*Belongings*

Tantamount relations between this star-crossed pair, things clearly were the opposite of fine

Contrary to their beliefs they made love after the first date

But Tommy was ever so forceful and Mischa became the victim of rape

He couldn't quench the urges to kiss her with a fist

Because the demons bottled up inside his brain were there to persist

The desire to start a family, a family Tommy never had

He outlived his mother and he outlived his dad

No excuses exercised, you can't use the old ruse of mental decline

Read between the sheets of his autobiography, atrophy like a venereal wine

Don't judge the book unless you can grow a backbone and a spine

Flashforward to Tommy's graveyard: Mischa stands statuesque, tears bleeding into her mascara

Just her and his ex-girlfriend; I think her name was Tara

Their eyes meet by the headstone and they both look down at their feet

*BLOOD/ SUGAR/ SEX/ TRAGIK*

As the eulogy is read out by the handsomest and holiest of the Catholic priests

The words come streaming out of the black hole and you'd fail to hear sounds cascade against the silence

"Here lies Tommy the Cunt. Rest in pieces the poster boy for domestic violence"

What's a little cash transaction between lovers - nothing

The spill of crimson between lovers after the fact - it means everything

He lied, he stole, he destroyed, he scolded, he ran rough shod on her misery

Blood sugar sugar blood sugar sugar blood blood

*"I object to violence because when it appears to do good, the good is only temporary; the evil it does is permanent."*

Mahatma Gandhi

*Belongings*

## Submissive Protocol Inc.

"I don't like the direction in which things are going"

She said as I was gnawing on a piece of rubble

When inert feelings compound the density growing

You knew my middle name was natural-born trouble

(Shout out B Dolan)

I sat two metres apart from your shadow

Not too be rude, just because lockdown had been tough

The touch paper of love just wasn't enough

The rabid stink of it called my bluff

Submissive Protocol Inc, it read on red-headed stationery

This modern sobriety thing has left me wanting and stationary

You broke the first rule of Fuck Club

Don't talk about Fuck Club

Our clandestine lust acting as a benign cyst

Removed by the pillars of solitude surrounding my reverie

*Submissive Protocol Inc.*

"Bastards will always be bastards"

He said, as he licked his lips with almighty dread

The noughts and crosses we played by the fireplace

Gave chase to the notion that sexuality is spectrum based

Then we washed down that analogy with a shot of Sambuca

I was 19. The other lads were out playing footy and doing the three-legged race

We were together getting smashed, obliterated, disgraced

But that kiss we had was something chaste and irreplaceable

At the time I thought thousands of normalities crashed down to jam the monotony

Of study into the cavernous soul I'd erased

Submissive Protocol Inc, the factory is open 24/7

Patchwork-quilted guilt over cheating on Stace

*Belongings*

## The Only Way Out Is Through

The only way out is through
With chaotic rage and repellent malaise
A labyrinth looks a bit like a brain
These are the things I think of at 4 am
The two hands aside my earlobes
And a signpost that screams "Shout, shout, let it all out"
The fears for tears became part of the zoo
The only way out is through

The only way out is through
In caps locks, enchantment is twice removed
Like a cousin at a party you'd secretly hate
Because the bartender is giving you the evil eye
Whilst you polish off a shit sandwich on a fucking paper plate
The clowns are all depressed
What a terrible fete
The moment you want to inform the screws
The only way out is through

*The Only Way Out Is Through*

The only way out is through

Problems do not maketh man nor boy

You told me Geronimo was the safe word

Whilst you crossed my horizons and flipped me the bird

I don't know where this poem is going; guess and give us a clue

The only way out is through


I've got diamonds and duct tape

Destitute illusions of grandeur

Six feet four and a fucking tantrum

(Use too many swears when I'm manic

Praying for a fugue state instead)

The tiara is overrated as is the halo

I'm waiting for death to deliver its payload

(Wish I was back in my childhood bedroom

Chilling with sock fights and SuperTed)

But in the meantime, I'll find a joy to imbue

The only way out is through

*Belongings*

The only way out is through

(... there's 2000 volts running through

2000 mirror reflections of self

There's 2021 years gone in the AD multiverse

There's ADHD and bi-polar and Asperger's in my stream

Wouldn't have it any other way for my creative streak but,

Sometimes it hurts being a human

When finding it hard to be humanitarian

Sometimes I don't fathom if I'm animal, mineral, vapor or steam

The world feels like an arcade game stuck in a daydream

There's 2000 jolts to the system

I want it out of my system

I insist babe, it's gruesome

Pedestrian and speeding

Watching the film of my life unspooling

The narrative gets me reeling

Continuity editing is a saving grace

But I continually chase my own ghost

*The Only Way Out Is Through*

Into the canyon of great noisy
Barren stables where I just love toast and Halsey
That's great and inspirational of a morning
But here's a red-eye storm warning
I may have only 5 more minutes to be bereft
So, I exist and exit stage left...)

*Belongings*

## Quantify Your Expectations (Bus Billboard)

A philosophical quandary

About quantifying your expectations

Do you need therapy cos the world is on fire?

Trapped under the wheels of a bus full of bison

Do you find retail consumer energy is a beacon of hope

Cos Black Friday is the day you can't find a way off the rope?

Attainment is beautiful when it's self-worth centric

I need your lip gloss kisses and mascara tantric splendid

Billboards selling the latest fresh commodity

They don't bring togetherness for such space oddities as you and I

They divide with tan lines and stretch marks and celluloid cellulite

We spin on IO, we chatter on IOS systems

Arachnid-like spiders weaving webs of hysteria

So, quantifying your expectations is nothing more than a present

Conundrum in bad weather, fleeting and irreverential

*Quantify Your Expectations (Bus Billboard)*

Pension schemes, pyramid dreams, arsonists of faith

You don't need gods and goddesses, you crave being mentally safe

Physically repugnant psychic bitches, by that I mean dogs

Bittersweet and in absolute stitches, turning the cogs

Society's burden is life, can't be preserved

When it ouroboros itself to a starving nation

*Belongings*

## Tastes Like Treason

A veneral thistle, guzzle the gristle
Stinging vipers with a political missile
Inverted commas and exclamation marks
The code they use when they describe the economic dark
Bigotry is bi and go with an added try
But the freedom percolated from a sinister lie
Greed follows greed, money hollows money
Bazooka the barricade with a meme that's funny
Something sweet to sharpen the saccharine
As they throw your personal pride into the acidic ravine
Whatever happened to the British (or even) the American Dream?
All of which are custard creams
All of which fall apart like fucking broken custard creams

Rage is having our backs against the wall, but hollering "you won't win"
Against- the anti- for we reassemble giving us hope to believe in

*Tastes Like Treason*

The is the prefix of The Good The Bad and The Ugly

Machines are killing us in the name of hope that once tasted lovely

Eurozone, they trying to send our Euros home

I bleed both British and Polish so suck my vehement bone

Headlines with no headroom make head-scratching hard

Because they chipped and pinned our hearts along with credit cards

"Sign on the dotted line... here's your special delivery"

An archaic sentiment fed to the dogs as consciousness(less) chivalry

The Union Jack represents a subliminal tack

False prophets for false profits, false patriotism smokes like false positive prolapse

Whatever happened to the Green Grass and Sunny Side of the Street?

Every hospital, school, church became a Nandos or a jungle of concrete

Every hospital, school, church became a Nandos or a fucking jungle obsolete

*Belongings*

Rage is having our backs against the wall, but hollering "you won't win"

Against- the anti- for we reassemble giving us hope to believe in

The is the prefix of The Good The Bad and The Ugly

Machines are killing us in the name of hope that once tasted lovely


Only fools back the horses that previously advertised glue

Opportunity knocks at the door and then proceeds to steal your shoes

This is your life for your husbands, wives, kids and absent friends

If you are what you eat, you ate the Kingdom you once over died to defend

Bankroll the meek, the weak, those who speak in common houses

It's tricky, kind of like when Blowback taught me 'bout Jamaican skirts and trousers

Our origins and roots maligned like the poor defenceless cat in that wheelie bin

So, sing a song a sixpence instead of singing a song of Vicodin and placebo vitamin

*Tastes Like Treason*

Bust the chops before they dust our shops

Detonate their sacrosanct before they flood our banks

Expel the education systems where textbook is king

Bust the chops before they dust our shops

Because we don't owe them anything

*Belongings*

## Do (Not) Resuscitate

I'm laid out bare on the operating table
My body fortunes the brave of another fickle fable
Living is just an endless quest for answers
From the cerebral cortex to the hippocampus

I put my faith in all of Western medicine
But all I got in return, the unwanted feeling, hypochondria
Side effects may include dizziness, tremors and inertia

There is no known cure for broken heart syndrome
My blood ran cold with loneliness and solitude
Could bleeding vessel be mended or was I to be eternally alone
I took comfort in having loved and lost
The cliche is true, love truly comes and goes

Wounds they heal and scars mostly fade
No cancers nor diseases can ail me

## Do (Not) Resuscitate

As long as there's breath in my lungs, I will strive to demonstrate
The strength to overcome all life's debilitating adversities

That 27-year itch is nearly over, I've made it this far
I'll admit sometimes I feared my mortality
Those before me made it close but no cigar
So, I'm glad last year I vanquished my insanity

Maybe I smoke too many cigarettes
Drink a little too much liquor
I'm a tad overweight
But chances are I'll live fast and die no quicker

If I ever make it to the hospital, in such a terminal state
Tell the doctors I lived a great long honest life
Do not resuscitate

Here's hoping when my days are numbered
And of living I'm pretty well fed
On my deathbed soapbox let my final words be

*Belongings*

A thank you to those close and the folks I've met
For the memories shared and the confidences kept
As the decades pass on by
With my health I may take more liberties
But I say fuck it and enjoy
Embrace the luxury of being free

When I'm too old and weary
Tomorrow's impossible to contemplate
I won't get emotional and teary
Let the so-called gods decide my fate
Even to a heathen unbeliever like me
It's a leap of faith I'll have to take
There'll be a sign on heaven's door
That reads "do not resuscitate"

## Luca

Luca
You are a blessed boy
Borne from the souls of two entwined humanoids
Little man with those mischievous eyes
You go to sleep, but your light still shines

A little glimmer of our Grandad's cheeky side
A smile so full, a hundred miles wide
I'm sure as you grow older, you'll allow your Mom and Dad some zeds
You see the world anew and on the screen us talking heads
A little dude with a future destiny like a goldmine
You go to sleep, but your light still shines

When I heard I was going to be an uncle
Was so excited to see your beautiful face
I knew you'd be a little heartbreaker
Treasured by all who meet you, by all who speak your name
I'll always be around to watch you grow

*Belongings*

We'll play football on sunny weekends, into the score sack the ball will go

You're so lucky with all the love from many families

Maybe one day you'll be a chef, an astronaut, a musician, so many opportunities

You'll be adored whatever path you decide

Go to sleep, little Luca, your light will always shine

## Until Next Time/ RU Not Entertained

Until next time
Blow a candle out as you remember me
All the best bits and the faults
Somersault in your memory bank
But whatever you do
Don't regret me
I was the man who made you laugh
I was the man behind the autograph
I dared to dream a gazillion dreams
I feared everyone and everything it seems, respectfully
Posthumously yours
I died not a martyr to a cause
I didn't die for your applause
Death just found me like it does us all
Until next time
Tell your friend or a lover
That I was a star in a darkened sky
Faded out and away before its time

*Belongings*

Yes, I did some things I wasn't best proud of
Yes, I made some claims I couldn't live up to
Though I lived ferociously and fearlessly
Against the tides that beckoned me
To self-immolate and burn like embers
In the disfigured dismembered bodies of enemies
Until next time
If there's an afterlife
Be I not human, that'd be sublime
Do not cry for me or lie for me
Do not die for nothing, live for every time
Because all we've got is now and that is fine
I hope you still remain in the cracks between the lines
Until next time…


We're not hear for you to use as totems
Dredging up our past indiscretions
Neither are we here for your enter-shame-ment
These are real issues, not tear-filled tissues of lies

If I drink too much, if he smokes too much

If she is promiscuous, if he looks vacuous

If they have a different vibe, embrace it

If their opinions differ, human up and face it

This isn't runaway train cannon fodder for the masses

We're not molasses in a highball glass to be coiffed by you bastards

Are you entertained? I hope not

These transmissions are to assuage you of your apathy

I don't want your love, but I don't want you to love to hate

It's a fate worse than nihilistic circumstantial lack of faith

These words and tales that twist like snakes up ladders doused in flame

We are one and individual, also we are one and the fucking same

Thrust into a whirlwind world as a mass of cells, it's a masochistic game

In the end we are just food for the worms beneath a shallow grave

*Belongings*

So whilst we've got the opportunity, let's live it up and dance in this ridiculous rave

It's a carnival of recriminations, cards on the table, show no shame

We are all just fucked up little fledglings here to masticate and maim

Life isn't kind to the rat race, live like a lion or risk being tamed...

The only way out is through, for one last time can you beat the maze?

Printed and bound by CPI Group (UK) Ltd, Croydon, CR0 4YY
13/02/2024
03698778-0001